Canadian Geography & Mapping Skills

Encouraging Topic Interest

Help students develop an understanding and appreciation of different types ... maps such as population maps, climate maps, topographical maps, etc. Tourism bureaus are great sources of free maps. Downloading maps from the Canada Website is also an option. In addition, encourage students to bring in a variety of maps to add to the class map collection. Examples of maps include road maps, tourist maps, neighbourhood maps, park maps, amusement park maps, floor plans, etc. Also have handy, atlases and other resources for further study.

Vocabulary List

Record new vocabulary of theme related words. In addition, keep track of new and theme related vocabulary on chart paper for students' reference during activities. Classify the word list into categories such as nouns, verbs, adjectives, or physical features.

Black Line Masters and Graphic Organizers

Use the black line masters and graphic organizers to present information, reinforce important concepts and to extend opportunities for learning. The graphic organizers will help students focus on important ideas, or make direct comparisons.

Outline Maps

Use the maps found in this teacher resource to teach the names, location of physical regions, provinces, territories, cities, physical features and other points of interest. Encourage students to create their own Canada atlas using the maps from this book and adding information reports.

Learning Logs

Keeping a learning log is an effective way for students to organize their thoughts and ideas about concepts presented. Student learning logs also give the teacher insight on what follow up activities are needed to review, and to clarify concepts learned.

Learning logs can include the following kinds of entries:

- teacher prompts
- student personal reflections
- questions that arise
- connections discovered
- labelled diagrams and pictures

Rubrics and Checklists

Use the rubrics and checklists in this book to assess student learning.

Table of Contents

The Seven Continents

This is a map of the world's seven continents and five oceans. Colour the map and complete the map legend.

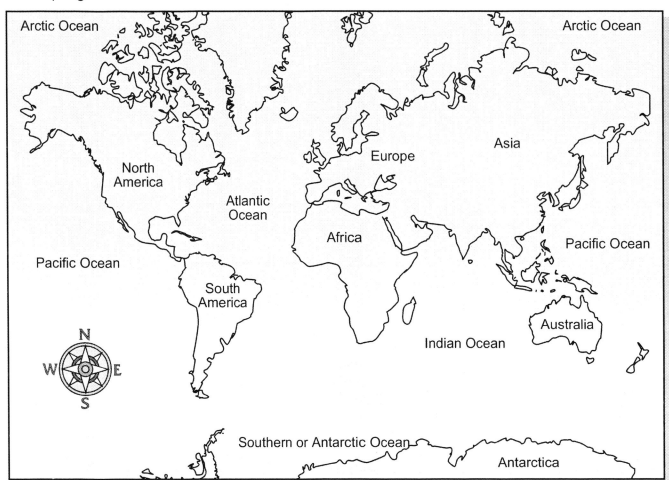

MAP LEGEND

Oceans	Europe	North America	South America	Asia	Africa	Australia	Antarctica

Brain Stretch

1. List the seven continents. _____

_____

2. List the five oceans. _____

3. What continent do you live on? _____

Canada

This is a map of Canada. A **map** is a flat drawing of a place.

Canada is the second largest country in the world. It has 10 provinces and 3 territories. Canada is on the continent of North America and borders three oceans. The Atlantic Ocean is on the east coast. The Pacific Ocean is on the west coast. The Arctic Ocean is on Canada's northern coast. The United States is Canada's neighbour to the south.

Fill in the blanks using information from the reading:

Canada is the _____ largest country in the _____. It has _____ provinces

and _____ territories. Canada is on the continent of _____

and borders three _____. The Atlantic Ocean is on the _____ coast.

The Pacific Ocean is on the _____ coast. The Arctic Ocean is on Canada's

_____ coast. The United States is Canada's _____ to the south.

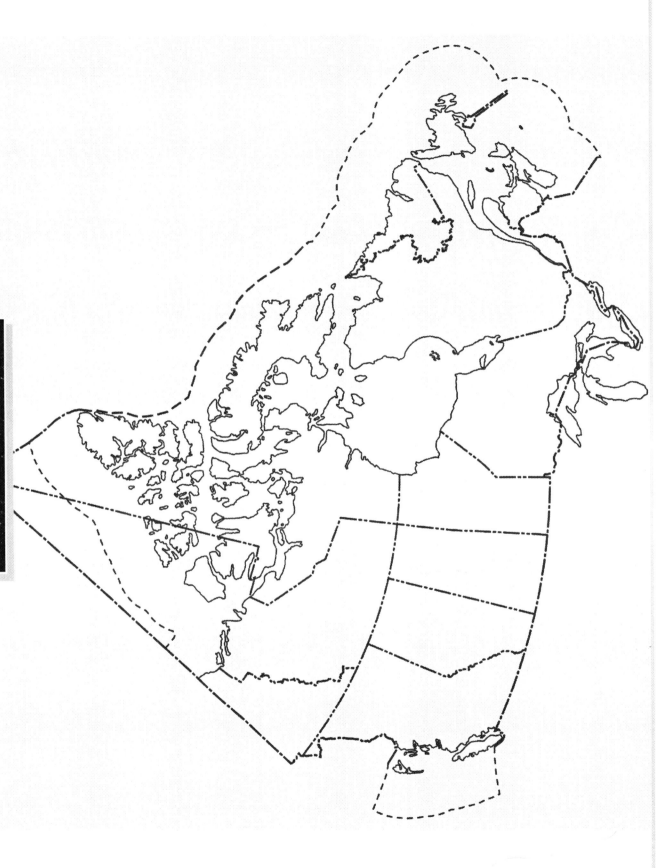

Canada's Physical Regions

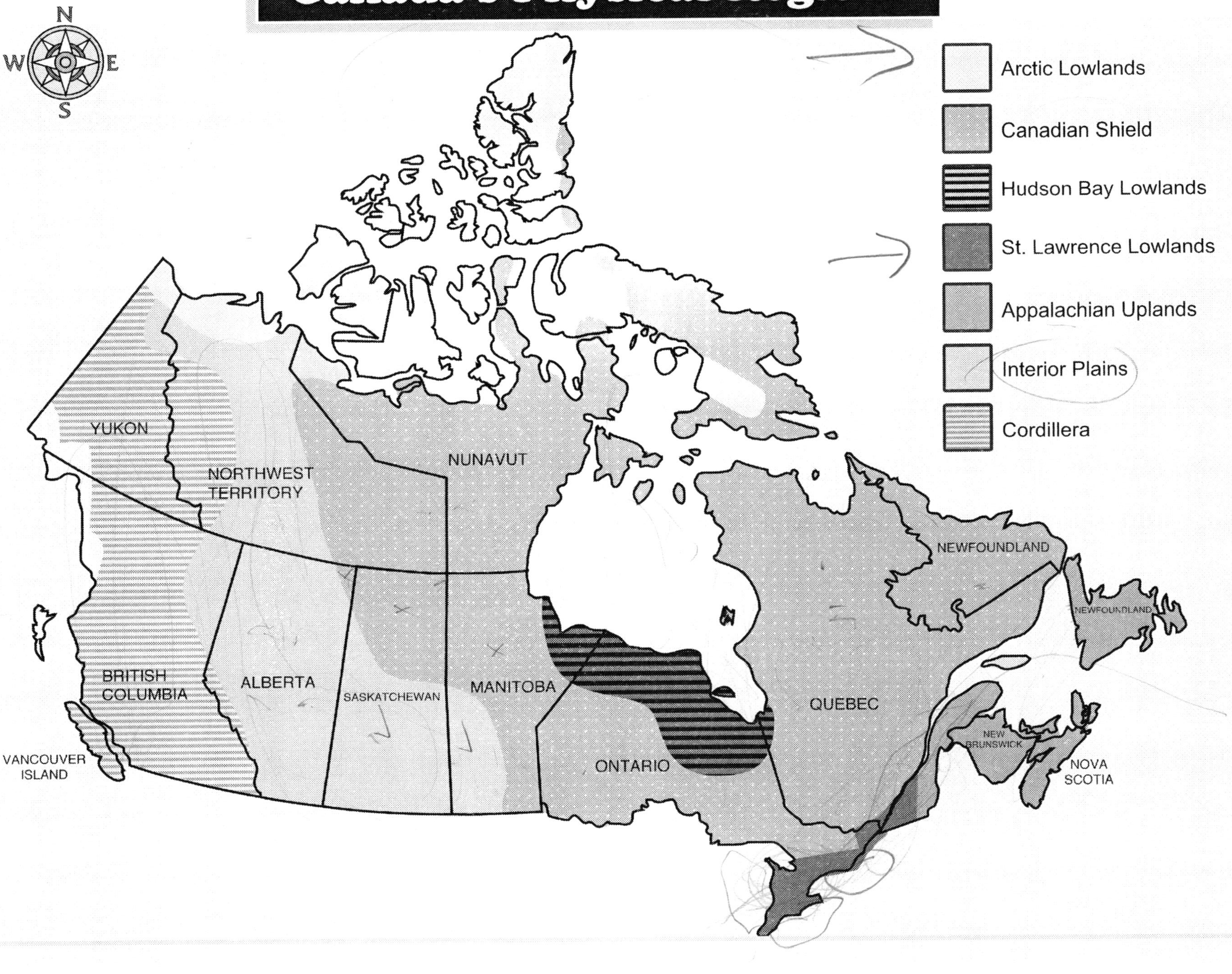

Arctic Lowlands

Canadian Shield

Hudson Bay Lowlands

St. Lawrence Lowlands

Appalachian Uplands

Interior Plains

Cordillera

NEWFOUNDLAND

NOVA SCOTIA

NEW BRUNSWICK

QUEBEC

ONTARIO

MANITOBA

SASKATCHEWAN

ALBERTA

NUNAVUT

NORTHWEST TERRITORY

YUKON

BRITISH COLUMBIA

VANCOUVER ISLAND

N E S W

The St. Lawrence Lowlands

Location

The St. Lawrence Lowlands includes part of the Ottawa River valley, Anticosti Island and part of the southern coast of Quèbec and Labrador. It also spans from Georgian Bay south to Niagara River in the Ontario and east along the St. Lawrence River to Quèbec.

Physical Features

NIAGARA FALLS

The St. Lawrence Lowlands region has both flat land and some hills. The rivers drain into the five Great Lakes and the St. Lawrence River. The five Great Lakes are Lake Superior, Lake Michigan, Lake Huron, Lake Erie, and Lake Ontario. There are islands in the Great Lakes. The plain around the Great Lakes was formed when particles of earth called sediment were carried by rivers and streams and settled. This plain has very deep and fertile soil.

The Niagara Escarpment is located near the Great Lakes. An **escarpment** is a long rocky cliff that marks the boundary of a flat or gently sloping upland area. The Niagara River flows over the escarpment at Niagara Falls.

Climate

For the most part, the St. Lawrence Lowlands have hot and humid summers. Winters are cool and are frequently snowy. The area near the Great Lakes has one of the longest growing seasons in Canada.

Vegetation

- The St. Lawrence Lowlands have mixed forests of coniferous and deciduous trees. Coniferous trees include fir, spruce and hemlock. Deciduous trees include sugar maple, walnut and oak.
- The St. Lawrence Lowlands have very fertile soil and some of the best growing areas in Canada.

Wildlife

- mammals such as white-tailed deer, squirrels, moose and lynx
- fish such as yellow perch and northern pike
- birds such as bluebirds, blackbirds, loons and woodpeckers

Natural Resources

- iron ore, zinc, silver, coal, copper and lead • fresh water • sugar maple trees • fertile soil for growing
- hydroelectricity

Chalkboard Publishing © 2009

The Interior Plains

Location

The Interior Plains region runs along the east side of the Cordillera and reaches as far north as the Arctic Ocean. It also includes large parts of Alberta, Saskatchewan and Manitoba as well as part of the Northwest Territories.

Physical Features

The Interior Plains region is very flat or has rolling hills. The land is at its highest level in the foothills of the Rocky Mountains. The land is almost at sea level in Manitoba and the Northwest Territories. Thousands of years ago, glaciers covered the Interior Plains and much of Canada.

The weight of the glaciers compressed the land and caused it to become flat with rolling hills. The glaciers left behind rock, silt, gravel and sand. Furthermore, as the glaciers melted, lakes and rivers were formed. The Interior Plains now include many of the largest and longest rivers in Canada.

The southern part of the Interior Plains has the largest area of farmland in Canada. The fertile soil is excellent for growing cereal grains such as wheat, oats, rye and barley.

Climate

Most areas of the Interior Plains have cold winters and hot summers. The Interior Plains region has the least amount of precipitation in Canada and in some areas can experience droughts. A **drought** occurs when there is no rain or snow for a long period of time. When there is drought, the grasses of the southern Interior Plains go dormant and wait to grow until there is rain. **Irrigation** is sometimes necessary to grow crops. Irrigation is a method of bringing water.

Vegetation

- Trees and shrubs grow along streams and near bodies of water.
- Most trees are deciduous.
- In the southern Interior Plains the natural vegetation is mostly grasses.
- In the northern part of the Interior Plains only small plants, mosses and grasses grow.

Wildlife

- birds such as ducks, geese and swans
- wolves and polar bears live in the north
- herbivores such as deer, moose, elf and caribou
- carnivores such as coyotes, eagles and hawks

Natural Resources

- coal and potash • oil and gas • fertile land in the southern part of the region • minerals

The Cordillera

Location

The Cordillera is a region of mountains found on the west side of Canada, next to the Pacific Ocean. The Cordillera region includes the province of British Columbia and some parts of the Yukon, Alberta and the Northwest Territories.

Physical Features

ROCKY MOUNTAINS

The Cordillera region includes many different landforms: mountains, hills, plateaus and valleys. There are also many different sized lakes and major river systems. The Fraser River system is the largest. There are also several mountain ranges in the Cordillera region including the Columbia Mountains, Rocky Mountains and the Coast Mountains.

These mountain ranges were formed millions of years ago, when enormous folds of rocks bent and crushed against each other.

Climate

In the northern part of the Cordillera region there are cold winters and cool summers. There are warmer temperatures in the southern part of the Cordillera region. Along the coast, there are mild winters, warm summers and ample rain. The ocean helps to keep areas near the coast cooler in the summer and warmer in the winter.

Vegetation

- Most forests in the Cordillera region are coniferous. The largest coniferous trees in Canada are found in the rainforest near the Pacific Coast.
- Many plants, shrubs, and trees grow larger on the coast compared to other places.
- There is little vegetation at the tops of the high mountains.
- Grassland is the natural vegetation of much of the interior plateau.

Wildlife

- polar bears and caribou in the far north
- birds such as eagles, ravens and owls
- marine life such as whales, sea lions and seals
- mammals such as deer, elk, and lynx
- fish such as salmon, trout, halibut and northern pike

Natural Resources

- forests • fish like salmon, halibut and herring • hydroelectricity • lead, sand and gravel
- Okanagan valley for growing fruit • gold, silver, copper and zinc

The Hudson Bay Lowlands

Location

The Hudson Bay Lowlands runs around the southern part of Hudson Bay and James Bay and includes parts of Manitoba, northern Ontario and Québec.

Physical Features

The Hudson Bay Lowlands was once part of Hudson Bay and is known as one of the flattest parts of Canada. The Hudson Bay Lowlands were created over long periods of time. As the glaciers from the Ice Age slowly melted away, the level of the land got higher. Since the land is near sea level, it is marshy and water does not drain away.

The Hudson Bay Lowlands region has the largest area of **wetlands** in the world. Wetlands are lands that are covered with water all or almost all of the time. Much of the Hudson Bay Lowlands has permafrost. It is called **permafrost** when the ground stays frozen all year round. Only the surface of the ground melts in the summer. Permafrost is another reason why the land does not drain away water easily.

Climate

The Hudson Bay Lowlands region has a climate very similar to the northern part of the Canadian Shield. The winters are long and cold. The summers are short and warm. Precipitation mostly falls as snow during the winter.

Vegetation

- The majority of the Hudson Bay Lowlands is muskeg or peat forming wetland.
- There are long marshes along the coastline of Hudson Bay and James Bay.
- In the south western part of the Hudson Bay Lowlands there are thick forests of trees such as white spruce, white birch and balsam poplar.

Wildlife

- birds such as snow geese, whistling swans, ducks, and loons
- sea life such as seals and walruses
- mammals such as caribou, Arctic foxes, weasels and polar bears

Natural Resources

- hydroelectricity

The Canadian Shield

Location

The Canadian Shield region includes parts of Alberta, Saskatchewan, Manitoba, Ontario, Québec, the Northwest Territories, Nunavut and Labrador. It is the largest geographic region of Canada and covers about half of Canada.

Physical Features

The Canadian Shield is made of rock and is covered in most places with a thin layer of soil. In many places, bare rock shows through. Landforms in the Canadian Shield include both flat areas and rocky hills. There are forests, tundra, and lowlands.

More than ¼ of the Canadian Shield's surface is covered by water. The Canadian Shield has thousands of lakes, rivers, streams and marshes. Some rivers flow towards the Hudson Bay. Other rivers flow into the Great Lakes and the St. Lawrence River.

Climate

The northern part of Canadian Shield has long and cold winters. The summers are short and warm. Precipitation is light with less than 300 mm of rain and snow each year. In the northern part of the Canadian Shield there is permafrost. The southern part of the Canadian Shield has cold and snowy winters, while the summers are warm. Precipitation is up to 1600 mm per year.

Vegetation

- In the northern part there is tundra vegetation such as small plants, mosses and low growing shrubs.
- The rocky areas of the Canadian Shield region are barren.
- There are boggy wetlands called muskeg between the rocky hills.
- Mixed deciduous and coniferous forests grow in the southern part of the region.

Wildlife

- mammals such as caribou, moose and deer
- birds such as ravens, loons and sparrows
- fish such as trout, bass, perch and pickerel
- insects such as black flies and mosquitoes

Natural Resources

- hydroelectricity • softwood and hardwood • gold, silver, asbestos, nickel, zinc, iron, copper and uranium

The Arctic Lowlands

Location

The Arctic Lowlands is a small region that includes numerous islands in the Arctic Ocean and part of the far northern coast of Canada. Parts of the Yukon Territory, the Northwest Territories and Nunavut are also in the region. Almost the entire Arctic Lowlands region is found north of the Arctic Circle. The Arctic Circle is 63.5°N latitude.

Physical Features

Thousands of years ago, the Arctic Lowlands were covered by glaciers. This period of time was called the Ice Age. The Arctic Lowlands are huge flat areas of rock and boggy plains. The ground below the surface remains frozen all year round. This is called **permafrost**. Only the surface of the ground thaws in the summer. The soil is thin and does not easily grow plants.

Pingos are a landform found in areas of the Arctic Lowlands with permafrost. **Pingos** are rounded hills with a core of solid ice. They slowly grow larger as more water freezes on the ice in the centre of the hill.

Sea ice forms in the winter. **Sea ice** is ice formed in the salt water oceans, seas and straits. In the summer the sea ice will melt and break up into floating sheets of ice. These sheets of ice are called **ice floes** and range in size from a few metres to many kilometres across.

Climate

The Arctic Lowlands region has short, but sunny summers with clear skies. In the middle of the summer the sun does not set. During the long winters, the Arctic Lowlands region is very cold. In the middle of the winter, the sun does not rise above the horizon at all. The Arctic Lowlands region receives very little precipitation. Rainfall is rare during the summer and there is not much snowfall during the winter.

The **Aurora Borealis**, also known as the Northern Lights, can be seen in the Arctic Lowlands region. This is when moving broad sheets of light streak across the dark sky as energy from the sun acts on particles in the air.

Vegetation

• The Arctic Lowlands consists of many large areas of tundra.
• Only small scattered flowering plants, low-growing shrubs and mosses grow.
• Some places in the Arctic Lowlands are barren and have very few living plants.

Wildlife

• marine life such as whales, seals and walruses
• mammals such as wolves, polar bears and arctic foxes
• birds in the summer such as loons, snow geese and snowy owls

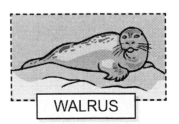
WALRUS

Natural Resources

• lead and zinc • coal • oil and natural gas • soapstone

The Appalachian Region

Location

The Appalachian region includes the provinces of New Brunswick, Nova Scotia, Prince Edward Island and Newfoundland. It also contains parts of Québec.

Physical Features

The Appalachian region is part of an ancient low range of mountains that have been worn down by erosion over millions of years. The Appalachian region is bordered by the Atlantic Ocean and has thousands of kilometres of sea coast. Waves, tides and swift ocean currents have eroded the cliffs and formed islands, beaches, bays and protected harbours. The Hopewell Rocks on the Bay of Fundy have some of the highest tides in the world.

HOPEWELL ROCKS

Off the shores of the Appalachian region, the ocean floor gradually slopes downward for many kilometres and suddenly drops off into a deep trench. This shallow extension near the land is known as the continental shelf. Those shallower portions of the shelf which lie southeast of Newfoundland are called the Grand Banks. The Grand Banks is world famous as a fishing ground. Fertile soils are found in some areas of the plains and valleys of the Appalachian region. The plains and valleys also have some areas that are very rocky.

Climate

The climate varies in the Appalachian region. Summers may be cool or warm and rainy. The winters are long and include much precipitation. In addition, during the winter the Northumberland Strait between P.E.I. and mainland freezes. Strong windstorms called gales are a regular occurrence.

Vegetation

• Coniferous trees such as black and white spruce and balsam fir grow both inland and on the coast of the Appalachian region.
• Trees grow slowly in the Appalachian region due to the rocky soil.
• Hardwood forests of beech, sugar maple and white birch have been almost completely logged.

Wildlife

• marine life such as grey seals and harbour seals
• mammals such as fox, deer, coyote, mink, hares, caribou and beaver
• fish such as cod, salmon and scallops
• birds such as puffins, gulls, blue herons and razorbills

Natural Resources

• oil • fish • zinc, lead, potash, salt • copper and gold

Canada's Physical Regions Brochure

Create a brochure for one of Canada's physical regions. A **brochure** is a booklet or pamphlet that contains descriptive information. The headings for the brochure are as follows:

- physical features
- climate
- vegetation
- wildlife
- natural resources
- interesting facts

Step 1: Plan Your Brochure

Step	Completion
1. Take a piece of paper and fold the paper the same way your brochure will be folded.	
2. Before writing the brochure, plan the layout in pencil. • Write the heading for each section where you would like it to be in the brochure. • Leave space underneath each section to write information. • Leave space for graphics or pictures.	

Step 2: Complete a Draft

Step	Completion
1. Research information for each section of your brochure.	
2. Read your draft for meaning and then add, delete or change words to make your writing better.	

Step 3: Final Editing Checklist

I checked for spelling _____

I checked for punctuation _____

I checked for clear sentences _____

My brochure is neat and organized _____

My brochure has pictures or graphics _____

My brochure is attractive _____

CANADA'S WILDLIFE

Canada is famous for its beautiful land and wildlife. The physical regions of Canada are diverse in many ways, including plant life, climate, landforms, natural resources and animals. Get information on Canada's wildlife at the following website:

www.hww.ca

Brain Stretch

Choose an animal from one of the physical regions of Canada. Present your findings in a booklet entitled: "All About the Canadian_____". Research the animal to find information about its:

- diet
- habitat
- adaptation to the region
- place in the food chain
- interesting facts

Important Tip! Make sure to include labelled diagrams and pictures!

CANADA'S RIVERS AND LAKES

Canada's rivers and lakes hold a lot of the world's freshwater. Freshwater is important because it is good to drink and sustains life. Learn more about the Great Lakes at the following website:

http://www.on.ec.gc.ca/greatlakes/default.asp?lang=En&n=4DB7BBAD-1

Learn more about the importance of freshwater at:

http://www.ec.gc.ca/water/e_main.html

Brain Stretch

- Make a list of the Great Lakes.
- Make a list of all of the ways water is used in daily life. What would happen if people did not have fresh water?
- What is Canada's longest river?

Canadian Match-Up

Match the provinces and territories to the names of their capital cities.

Nunavut	Victoria
Ontario	Halifax
Québec	Fredericton
Alberta	Toronto
Saskatchewan	Winnipeg
Northwest Territories	Edmonton
Nova Scotia	Whitehorse
Newfoundland and Labrador	Québec City
New Brunswick	Regina
Prince Edward Island	St. John's
British Columbia	Iqaluit
Yukon	Yellowknife
Manitoba	Charlottetown

Nickname: Garden of the Gulf

Land Area: 5660 square km of land

Physical Region(s): Appalachian region

Capital City: Charlottetown

Main Communities: Charlottetown and Summerside

Provincial Flower: Lady's Slipper

Provincial Bird: Blue Jay

www.gov.pe.ca

Prince Edward Island (P.E.I.) joined confederation on July 1, 1873 and was named after the father of Queen Victoria of Britain. P.E.I. is known as the birthplace of Canadian Confederation. Sir John A. MacDonald and his colleagues met in Charlottetown to develop the ideas that would lead to the union of Canada's early provinces into one country.

Location

Found on the east coast of Canada, Prince Edward Island (P.E.I.) is the smallest and only island of the provinces and territories. It is also an Atlantic province. To the west is the province of New Brunswick and Nova Scotia is in the south. The Gulf of St. Lawrence surrounds P.E.I. on three sides

Landscape

P.E.I. is 224 kilometres long with many sandy beaches, sandy marshes and sand dunes. The Gulf of St. Lawrence surrounds P.E.I. on three sides. There is no place in the province that is more than 16 km from the sea. Many small islands are located off P.E.I's shores.

Industries

The main industries in P.E.I. include agriculture, tourism, fisheries, and light manufacturing. The red soil of the island made from red sandstone produces one of P.E.I.'s major exports: potatoes. Other people in P.E.I. work as Irish moss harvesters. Irish moss is algae. Its extract is used in many products like ice cream, beer, and cosmetics. P.E.I. is also known for lobsters, scallops, mussels, oysters and potatoes.

Natural Resources

• fertile soil • Irish moss • fish, lobster and shellfish • woodlots

Atlantic Province: Nova Scotia

Nickname: Canada's Ocean Playground

Land Area: 55 500 square km of land

Physical Region(s): Appalachian region

Capital City: Halifax

Main Communities: Halifax, Dartmouth, Lunenburg, Sydney

Provincial Flower: Mayflower

Provincial Bird: Osprey

www.gov.ns.ca

Nova Scotia was one of the original four provinces to join confederation on July 1, 1867. Nova Scotia means New Scotland, and was first settled by people from Scotland.

Location

Nova Scotia is an Atlantic province. To the northwest is the province of New Brunswick. Prince Edward Island is to the north. To the northeast is Newfoundland and Labrador.

Landscape

Nova Scotia has two parts: the mainland and Cape Breton Island. Cape Breton Island is connected to Nova Scotia by the Canso Causeway. The Atlantic Ocean, the Bay of Fundy and the Northumberland Strait surround Nova Scotia. It also has numerous inlets, small islands, coves and bays in addition to a rocky coastline. Nova Scotia is visited by many migrating birds since it is approximately mid way between the Equator and the North Pole.

Industries

Some of the main industries in Nova Scotia include manufacturing, fishing, mining, tourism, agriculture, and forestry. Nova Scotia's "fish farms" include Atlantic salmon, blue mussels, American and European oysters and rainbow trout. Nova Scotia's Annapolis Valley and the northern part of the province are where dairy farms, poultry farms, fruit farms and vegetable farms are found.

Natural Resources

• softwood and hardwood forests • coal mining • gypsum • salt, sand and gravel
• inshore and offshore fishing • hydroelectricity

Atlantic Province: New Brunswick

Nickname: The Picture Province

Land Area: 72 000 square km of land

Physical Region(s): Appalachian region

Capital City: Fredericton

Main Communities: Saint John, Moncton, Fredericton, and Bathurst

Provincial Flower: Purple Violet

Provincial Bird: Black-capped Chickadee

www.gov.nb.ca

New Brunswick was one of the original four provinces to join confederation on July 1,1867. Originally, Samuel de Champlain and the French settled in what is now called Acadia in 1608. This east coast area is still predominantly French speaking. New Brunswick was named after the royal family of King George III, the house of Brunswick.

Location

New Brunswick is an Atlantic province. Prince Edward Island is its neighbour to the east, with Québec to the north and Nova Scotia to the south.

Landscape

New Brunswick's main features include mountains in the north, thick forests covering most of the province, as well as lakes and rivers formed during the last ice age. Hopewell Rocks on the Bay of Fundy is a popular tourist destination in New Brunswick. At Hopewell Rocks large "flower pots" can be seen. These "flower pots" are where the ocean has carved unique shapes from the seabed. The Bay of Fundy has the highest tides every day. There are two high tides and two low tides every day.

Industries

Main industries in New Brunswick include manufacturing, fishing, mining, forestry service and pulp and paper. Some people also work at bilingual call centres. This is where Canadians call to reach 800 phone numbers for information. New Brunswick is also known for growing potatoes and fruit such as apples, blueberries, strawberries and cranberries. Grand Manan is a well-known fishing port in New Brunswick.

Natural Resources

• peat moss • metals like lead, copper, silver and zinc • potash • forests • fishing

Nickname: The Rock

Land Area: 371 700 square km of land

Physical Region(s): Canadian Shield, St. Lawrence Lowlands

Capital City: St. John's

Main Communities: St John's, Corner Brook and Gander

Provincial Flower: Pitcher Plant

Provincial Bird: Atlantic Puffin

www.gov.nf.ca

Newfoundland and Labrador is the most eastern Atlantic province in Canada. It was the last province to join confederation on March 31, 1949.

Location

Newfoundland is an island with Labrador attached to the mainland. It is the most easterly province. Québec is its neighbour to the west. Nova Scotia is its neighbour to the southwest. The Gulf of St. Lawrence, the Atlantic Ocean, and the Arctic Ocean surround the island of Newfoundland. To travel to the island, people must fly in on an airplane, or take a ferry.

Landscape

Newfoundland and Labrador's main physical features include mountains and hills, plateaus, uplands and lowlands. Its rocky coastline contains many bays and fiords. Most of Labrador is in the Canadian Shield and has many forests. Some of these forests are lichen forests. The ground between the trees is covered with lichens and mosses. Other large areas of Labrador are covered by swamp and muskeg. The northern part of Labrador is tundra with flat treeless plains. Newfoundland is home to the Grand Banks. The Grand Banks are shallow waters to the east and south of Newfoundland. Some of the richest fishing grounds in the world are found in the Grand Banks.

Industries

Hydro-electricity, mining iron ore, manufacturing pulp and paper, tourism, and fishing are important industries in Newfoundland. Service is also a major industry for Newfoundland and Labrador.

Natural Resources

• uranium, nickel, gold, iron, copper, lead and zinc • offshore petroleum • Grand Banks- fish • hydroelectricity

Central Province: Québec

Nickname: La belle province
(The Beautiful Province)

Land Area: 1.4 million square km of land

Physical Region(s): Canadian Shield, Applachian, St. Lawrence Lowland

Capital City: Québec City

Main Communities: Québec City, Montreal, Sherbrooke, Hull, and Trois-Rivières

Provincial Flower: White Lilly

Provincial Bird: Snowy Owl

www.gov.nb.ca

Québec is the largest province in Canada and was one of the original four provinces to join confederation on July 1, 1867. The province takes its name from the Algonquin people's word for "the place where the river narrows". Most people in Québec speak French.

Location

Québec is a central province and is surrounded by water on three sides. Ontario is Québec's neighbour to the west. Newfoundland and Labrador are located to the northeast and New Brunswick to the southeast.

Landscape

Almost half of Québec is covered with trees and boasts numerous lakes and rivers. The landscape also includes plains, mountains, hills and plateaus. The Canadian Shield covers the majority of the province. The Canadian Shield is made up of rock, forests, mountains, lakes and wetlands. The majority of Québec's population lives in the St. Lawrence Lowlands region.

Industries

Québec is the largest producer of maple syrup in the world. Québec also has more dairy farms than any other Canadian province. Cheeses made in Québec are favourites worldwide and have won many awards. Other industries in Québec include manufacturing, agriculture, electricity production, mining, pulp and paper, meat processing, and petroleum refining. Québec is also known for making paper, boxes, tissue and newsprint.

Natural Resources

• iron ore • forests • gold • copper, zinc and lead • hydroelectricity • asbestos

Nickname: The Heartland of Canada

Land Area: 891 200 square km of land

Physical Region(s): Canadian Shield, Hudson Bay Lowlands and St. Lawrence Lowlands

Capital City: Toronto, the most populous city in the country

Main Communities: Toronto, Ottawa, Hamilton, London, Windsor, Oshawa, Sudbury, Kingston, Timmins and Thunder Bay.

Provincial Flower: Trillium

Provincial Bird: Common Loon

www.gov.on.ca

Ontario is the second largest province and was one of the original four provinces to join confederation on July 1, 1867. The name Ontario comes from an Iroquoian word meaning 'beautiful lake'.

Location

Ontario is a central province. Québec borders the east of Ontario and Manitoba borders the west. Hudson Bay is found to the north of Ontario, while the Great Lakes and the United States form the southern border.

Landscape

Almost half of Ontario is covered by the Canadian Shield. The Canadian Shield has jagged landforms, and fast flowing rivers. The southern region of Ontario lies in the St. Lawrence Lowlands. Here the climate is mild and the soil is exceptional for growing. The Niagara Escarpment is a limestone ridge that runs from Niagara Falls to Manitoulin Island. Four of the five Great Lakes are found in Ontario and along with the St. Lawrence River, create a waterway that transports much of Canada's grain, minerals and newsprint.

Industries

The main industries in Ontario include manufacturing, finance, construction, tourism, agriculture, mining, automotive and forestry. Some people work at federal government offices in Ottawa. Ontario's Niagara fruit belt is known for growing fruit such as grapes, peaches and apples.

Natural Resources

• soft and hardwood trees • petroleum • iron, copper, lead, gold, silver, nickel and zinc • fertile soil • water

Prairie Province: Saskatchewan

Nickname: The Breadbasket of Canada

Land Area: 570 700 square km of land

Physical Region(s): Interior Plains, Canadian Sheild

Capital City: Regina

Main Communities: Saskatoon, Regina, Prince Albert, and Moose Jaw.

Provincial Flower: Prairie Lilly

Provincial Bird: Sharp-tailed Grouse

www.gov.sk.ca

Saskatchewan joined confederation on July 1, 1905 and is one of Canada's Prairie Provinces. Saskatchewan comes from the Plains First Nations word "kisiskatchewan" which means "the river flows swiftly".

Location

Saskatchewan is in the centre of Canada. Saskatchewan is the only province in Canada to have completely man-made borders. To the east and west are the provinces of Manitoba and Alberta. To the north are the Northwest Territories and Nunavut.

Landscape

Saskatchewan has three main landforms: plains, thick forest and large rock formations. Almost one third of Saskatchewan is farmland. Saskatchewan is rich with forests and has over 100 000 freshwater lakes, river and bogs.

Industries

Saskatchewan's industries include ranching, agriculture, mining, meat processing, electricity production, petroleum refining and services. Saskatchewan is known for its farming and grows wheat for Canadians and other countries around the world. Saskatchewan is also the largest producer of potash and uranium in the world. Potash is used to help fertilize crops while uranium helps to produce electricity.

Natural Resources

• agricultural land • minerals such as potash, salt, uranium, petroleum • copper, zinc, nickel

Prairie Province: Alberta

Nickname: Sunny Alberta

Land Area: 644 000 square km of land

Physical Region(s): Interior Plains, Cordillera region

Capital City: Edmonton

Main Communities: Edmonton, Calgary, Lethbridge, Red Deer, Medicine Hat

Provincial Flower: Wild Rose

Provincial Bird: Great Horned Owl

www.gov.ab.ca

Alberta joined confederation on September 1st, 1905. It was named after a British princess and is one of the Prairie Provinces.

Location

Alberta is a prairie province. Alberta borders on British Columbia to the west and Saskatchewan to the east. The Northwest Territories is its neighbour to the north.

Landscape

Alberta's landforms include plains, mountains, foothills and badlands. Most of Alberta's land is made up of plains. There are grassland plains in the southeast and parkland plains in central Alberta. The magnificent Rocky Mountains run along Alberta's western border. Along the Red Deer River near Drumheller are Alberta's Badlands where hoodoos can be found. **Hoodoos** are pointed or flat-topped sandstone pillars. In addition, numerous dinosaur bones and fossils have been found in Alberta's badlands. Northern Alberta is forested and has many lakes and rivers.

Industries

The main industries in Alberta include mining, agriculture, beef ranching, manufacturing, finance and construction. Alberta is known for growing crops like wheat, barley and oats. Alberta is the main producer of oil, natural gas and coal in Canada. Other people work in the technology and research industry. Some people also work as part of the tourism industry.

Natural Resources

• land for farming or ranching • forests • oil, gas and coal • hydroelectricity

Prairie Province: Manitoba

Nickname: The Keystone Province

Land Area: 548 000 square km of land

Physical Region(s): Interior Plains, Canadian Shield and Hudson Bay Lowlands

Capital City: Winnipeg

Main Communities: Winnipeg, Brandon, Thompson, Portage la Prairie

Provincial Flower: Prairie Crocus

Provincial Bird: Great Grey Owl

www.gov.mb.ca

Manitoba joined confederation on July 15, 1870. Its name is a Cree word meaning the "place where the spirit speaks". Manitoba is home to many Métis, Aboriginal peoples, and other people from around the world. Many people in Manitoba speak English and French.

Location

Manitoba is a prairie province. It is the geographic centre of Canada. To the west is the province of Saskatchewan, to the east is the province of Ontario, and to the north is the territory of Nunavut.

Landscape

Lakes and rivers cover about one sixth of Manitoba. Lake Winnipeg is Canada's fifth largest lake. In the farthest areas of the north, the tundra landscape consists of short trees, swamps and large rock formations. The region of the province to the south is a flat, low-lying plain. The central and northern parts of the province are in the Canadian Shield. Wetlands and coniferous forests cover the Hudson Bay Lowlands. Churchill, Manitoba, a deep-sea port in Hudson Bay, is the best place in the world to see polar bears that migrate from the arctic in the winter time.

Industries

Main industries in Manitoba include manufacturing, agriculture, meat processing and mining. The Royal Canadian Mint in Winnipeg is where Canadian coins are made.

Natural Resources

• hydroelectricity • tantalum • agricultural land • nickel, gold, silver, copper, zinc and lead

Yukon Territory

Nickname: North 60

Land Area: 483 000 square km of land

Physical Region(s): Cordillera and Arctic Lowlands regions

Capital City: Whitehorse

Main Communities: Whitehorse, Dawson City, Watson Lake, Old Crow (the only settlement in the Yukon that is north of the Arctic Circle.)

Provincial Flower: Fireweed

Provincial Bird: Common Raven

www.gov.yk.ca

On June 13, 1898, the Yukon joined confederation and became Canada's second territory. The name Yukon comes from a Native word meaning 'great river.'

Location

The Yukon is the smallest of Canada's three territories and is located partly in the Arctic Circle in the northwest corner of the Far North. British Columbia is its neighbor to the south, the Northwest Territories on the east, and the U.S. state of Alaska on the west. North of the Yukon is the Beaufort Sea.

Landscape

The Yukon attracts visitors to explore its natural landscape, and to witness the Aurora Borealis. Mount Logan is the highest mountain in Canada and is found in Kluane National Park, within the St. Elias mountain ranges. The largest non-polar ice field in the world is also located in the St. Elias mountain ranges. The icefield is 700 metres thick, and is located in the heart of the mountains.

Industries

Industries in the Yukon include forestry, construction, manufacturing, fur trapping and tourism. The Yukon is recognized for the mining of natural resources including gold, silver, lead, oil and zinc. Tourism is of key importance to the Yukon and provides many service jobs in hotels, stores, restaurants, outdoor tour companies and transportation.

Natural Resources

• lead, zinc, gold, silver and copper • coal

Nickname: Beautiful BC

Land Area: 930 000 square km of land

Physical Region(s): Cordillera region

Capital City: Victoria, located on Vancouver Island

Main Communities: Vancouver, Victoria, Prince George, Kamloops, Kelowna, Nanaimo and Penticton.

Provincial Flower: Pacific Dogwood

Provincial Bird: Stellar's Jay

www.gov.bc.ca

British Columbia joined Confederation on July 20, 1871. The name British Columbia was chosen by Queen Victoria.

Location

British Columbia is the most western province located on the Pacific Coast. It has a mainland and many small islands. These islands include Vancouver Island and the Queen Charlotte Islands. British Columbia's neighbours are the Yukon and Northwest Territories in the north, the Pacific Ocean in the west and Alberta in the east.

Landscape

British Columbia has three main landforms: mountains, plains, and plateaus. The Coast mountains have some of the highest peaks in North America. The rocky mountains have thick forests and clear lakes. Half of the province is forested and is home to some of the largest and oldest trees in the world. British Columbia also has many rivers, lakes and waterfalls. British Columbia's Okanagan Valley has excellent growing conditions.

Industries

The industries in British Columbia include forestry, mining, tourism, agriculture, fishing, and manufacturing. British Columbia's Okanagan Valley is well known for growing fruit such as apples, plums and cherries. British Columbia is also known for developing computer software. The city of Vancouver is often called, "Hollywood North" because many films and TV shows are filmed there.

Natural Resources

• hydroelectricity • coal • gypsum and gravel • oil and natural gas • gold, lead, zinc and silver • lumber

Northwest Territories

Nickname: Land of the Midnight Sun

Land Area: 3.3 million square km of land

Physical Region(s): Cordillera, Arctic Lowlands, Interior Plains and Canadian Shield regions

Capital City: Yellowknife

Main Communities: Yellowknife, Hay River, Inuvik and Fort Smith

Provincial Flower: Mountain Avens

Provincial Bird: Gyrfalcon

www.gov.nt.ca

Northwest Territories (N.W.T.) is the second largest territory in Canada. It joined confederation on July 13, 1870 to become Canada's first territory.

Location

The Northwest Territories (N.W.T.) stretch north from the British Columbia, Alberta, and Saskatchewan borders and extend all the way to the Arctic Ocean and the high Arctic islands. East to west, it runs from the Nunavut boundary to the Mackenzie Mountains and the Yukon border.

Landscape

Most of the N.W.T is sub arctic country but includes mountains, forests and tundra. N.W.T. is home to the Mackenzie River, the longest river in Canada, as well as Great Bear Lake, one of the largest lakes in the world. The N.W.T. is an excellent place to witness the Aurora Borealis (also known as the Northern Lights.)

Industries

Industries in N.W.T. include services, trapping, mining, forestry, tourism, oil and gas, as well as arts and crafts. The Beaufort Sea and the Mackenzie River delta are areas that are under exploration. Large oil fields lie below these areas and oil companies have been trying to develop the region since the 1970's.

Natural Resources

• oil and gas • uranium, copper, • lead and zinc • diamonds

Nunavut Territory

Nickname: Nunuvut means, "Our Land"

Land Area: 2 million square km of land (land/water)

Physical Region(s): Canadian Shield, Arctic Lowlands

Capital City: Iqaluit

Main Communities: Iqaluit, Rankin Inlet, Arviat and Cambridge Bay

Provincial Flower: Purple saxifrage

www.gov.nu.ca

Nunavut is the newest and largest territory in Canada. It joined confederation on April 1, 1999 and was formed out of the Northwest Territories. Most residents in Nunavut are of Inuit descent.

Location

The eastern borders of Nunavut are the Atlantic Ocean and Hudson Bay. To the north, Nunavut borders on Baffin Bay and Greenland. The Northwest Territories and the Arctic Ocean make up its western border. To the south is the province of Manitoba.

Landscape

Nunavut is home to seven of Canada's largest islands and two thirds of Canada's coastline. It has many islands, including Baffin and Ellesmere Islands. Nunavut is one of the least populated areas in the world. Airplanes are the major source of travel in Nunavut and every community has an airstrip. Airplanes are used to transport people, food, machines or other materials to the areas of Nunavut. The water that is available in Nunavut is frozen for most of the year. The Aurora Borealis (Northern Lights) can be easily seen throughout Nunavut.

Industries

Much of the industry in Nunavut is tourism, hunting, trapping, mining and fishing. Nunavut is also known for its artists who create fine arts and crafts. Arctic animals such as caribou, polar bears, whales and seals are an important part of the Inuit culture. Tourists to Nunavut can experience adventures such as floe edge tours, canoeing, sea kayaking, hiking, backpacking, wildlife, whale watching and other cultural experiences.

Natural Resources

• oil and gas • uranium, copper, lead and zinc • diamonds

Comparing Provinces or Territories

LOCATION		
LANDSCAPE		
INDUSTRIES		
NATURAL RESOURCES		

Urban & Rural Communities

A community is a place where people live, work and share the same interests. When people live in a <u>village</u>, <u>reserve</u> or <u>hamlet</u> it is called a <u>rural community</u>. When people live in a <u>town</u>, <u>city</u> or <u>suburb</u> it is called an <u>urban community</u>. Some communities are smaller like the town of Fox Creek, Alberta. Some communities are very large like the city of Toronto, Ontario.

Rural Communities

Rural communities are usually small and have less traffic than towns or cities. People usually live spread out from each other and there is lots of open space. Some people in rural communities work in jobs related to farming, forestry, mining or fishing.

Urban Communities

Urban communities usually have lots of people, buildings, stores, and traffic. People usually live near each other in houses, duplexes or apartment buildings.

Brain Stretch

1. Using information from the reading and your own ideas, explain the kind of community you live in.

The Features of a Community

Community Name_____

Location of Community	
What kind of community is it?	
What natural resources or physical features are there?	
How are the land and natural resources used?	
What kinds of structures are in this community?	
What kind of transportation is available in this community?	

Urban and Rural Living

Reasons for Living in an Urban Area	Reasons for Living in a Rural Area

FIRST NATIONS COMMUNITIES

First Nations communities are located in both rural and urban areas across Canada. First Nations communities are called Indian reserves. An Indian reserve is land saved for the use of status Indians. Status Indians are people who are registered under the Indian Act.

Each First Nations community is unique. There are big communities and there are small communities. Each community shows its specific culture, traditions and language. Some First Nations communities are known for being a part of an industry like forestry or oil.

Visit the following website to learn about First Nations Communities.

http://www.aboriginalcanada.com/firstnation/

Brain Stretch

- Why do you think it is important that each community show its specific culture, traditions and language?

CITIES

Cities can be different sizes and change over time. People in cities usually live in houses, apartment buildings, townhouses, duplexes or other buildings. Most cities have some kind of industry such as manufacturing, stores, government buildings, hospitals, museums, shopping malls, sports arenas and schools. Each province has a capital city. The capital city of Canada is Ottawa, Ontario.

Go to the following website and learn more about Canada's provincial capital cities websites.

http://www.capitaleducanada.gc.ca/ccco/index_e.asp

Brain Stretch

- In your opinion, why do you think people may prefer to live in a city instead of another kind of community?

PORT COMMUNITIES

Some Canadians live in port communities. A port is a harbour or place for ships to dock and unload. Port communities are important for the transfer of goods such as grains or mineral ore. They help transport these things from community to community. Some of this cargo is then delivered across Canada and other parts of North America by trains, trucks or airplanes. Well known Canadian port cities include: Montreal, Québec; Vancouver, British Columbia; Halifax, Nova Scotia; Québec City, Québec; St. John's, Newfoundland; and Churchill, Manitoba. Port cities can be found on the east coast, west coast, Hudson Bay and along the St. Lawrence River. Visit this website to learn about the St. Lawrence Seaway system.

http://www.greatlakes-seaway.com/en/home.html

Brain Stretch

• How do you think port communities affect the lives of people in other communities?

FISHING COMMUNITIES

Some Canadians live in fishing communities. Canada is home to the Great Lakes and has the world's longest coastline. Some fishing communities have large ports with transportation connections, large fish processing plants, shipyards, and fish research facilities. Other fishing communities are very small and have small anchorages where boats are pulled onto the beach. The Canadian fisheries department decides how many fish can be caught. This is to prevent over fishing. When over fishing happens, nature cannot replace all the fish caught quickly enough. The Canadian government also protects the fishing industry by preventing other countries from fishing within 200 nautical miles of Canada's coast.

Learn more about Canada's oceans at this government website.

http://www.dfo-mpo.gc.ca/canwaters-eauxcan/bbb-lgb/index_e.asp

Brain Stretch

• Make list of types of fish and seafood caught in Canada.
• How do you think fishing communities affect the lives of people in other communities?

MANUFACTURING COMMUNITIES

Many Canadians live in manufacturing communities. The word manufacture means to make a completed product using raw materials. Some examples of manufactured goods are: cars, televisions, furniture, food products, toys or bubble gum. Usually, in a manufacturing community people work at a factory or plant. Not all people at the plant work to build something. Some people work at a plant or factory to supply services to other workers. These services include medical, social, security and food services.

Visit the following website to see how a factory produces bubble gum.

http://www.dubblebubble.com/tour.html

Brain Stretch

- Why do you think there are so many different workers in a manufacturing community? Explain your thinking.

- How do you think manufacturing communities affect the lives of people in other communities? Explain your thinking.

FORESTRY COMMUNITIES

Some Canadians live in forestry communities. Forestry means the cutting down and replanting of trees. Trees are natural resources that are used to make wood products such as paper or lumber for building. Usually people in a forestry community have jobs that are centred on forestry. One of the important jobs in a forestry community is the replanting of trees so that this natural resource does not run out.

Go to the kids' section of the Saskatchewan Forestry Association website to learn more.

http://www.whitebirch.ca/kids/kids.shtml

Brain Stretch

- Using your ideas, explain why it is important to replant trees.

- How do you think forestry communities affect the lives of people in other communities?

CANADIAN FARMING COMMUNITIES

Canada has many farming communities. Usually, neighbours in a farming community live quite a distance from each other. Stores, hospitals, or places to sell crops are usually located in a nearby town. Sometimes a farming community includes a town and the farms that surround the town. Canada has many types of farms such as dairy, vegetable, cattle, poultry, fruit and fish.

To learn more about different kinds of farming and how farming affects our daily lives, go the following website.

http://www.ext.vt.edu/resources/4h/virtualfarm/main.html

Brain Stretch

- What kind of farm would you like to have? Explain your thinking.

- How do you think farming communities are important to people who live in other communities? Explain your thinking.

MINING COMMUNITIES

Canada has many mining communities. Mining is the removal of minerals and metals from the earth. Some types of mines in Canada include gold, silver, zinc, nickel, lime and salt. Most people who live in a mining community work for the mining company in some way such as in the mine, in the mining offices or the company cafeteria.

Go to this website to find out where there are mining communities in Canada.

http://mmsd1.mms.nrcan.gc.ca/mmsd/producers/default_e.asp

Take a tour and identify how minerals are used in many household items.

http://www.nrcan.gc.ca/mms/wealth/intro-e.htm

Brain Stretch

- How do you think mining communities affect the daily lives of people in other communities? Explain your thinking.

CREATE AN URBAN COMMUNITY MAP

On grid paper, create a map of an urban community. Think about including things like:

highways	public places	apartment buildings	roads
houses	stores	school	hospital
factory	sanitation plant	physical features	government buildings

Brain Stretch

- Why might people who live in a rural community want to visit an urban community? Explain your thinking.
- Complete a community profile to tell about your urban community.

CREATE A RURAL COMMUNITY MAP

On grid paper create a map of a rural community. Think about including things like:

highways	farms	forest	school
houses	farm fields	stores	physical features
orchards	hospital		

Brain Stretch

- Why might people who live in an urban community want to visit a rural community? Explain your thinking.
- Complete a community profile to tell about your rural community.

Compass Rose

A **compass rose** is a design on a map that assists the map reader in finding directions. A compass rose shows the four cardinal directions. They are north, south, east and west. Sometimes a compass rose will also show northeast, northwest, southeast, and southwest. Mark the directions on the compass rose.

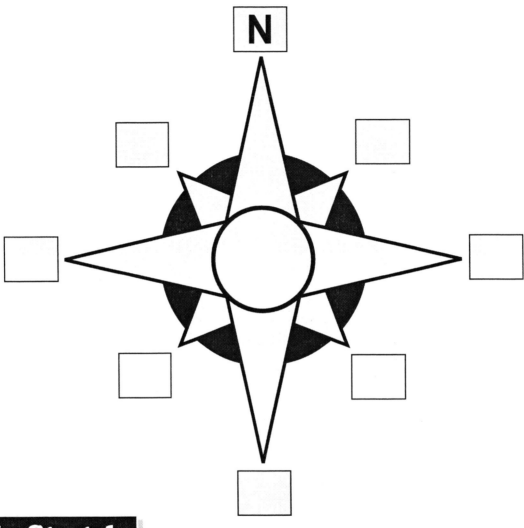

Brain Stretch

Using your own ideas, why do you think a compass rose is helpful?

Reading a Map

A **map** is a flat drawing of an area. A map is an important tool that assists people in finding the location of a place or thing.

TITLE • Every map has a **title**. A title tells the map reader what the map is about.	**A Map of Canada**
BOUNDARY • A **boundary** is a border or line on a map that outlines a political region like a country or province.	
LABEL • **Labels** on a map tell the map reader the names of places, points of interest and physical features like names of rivers, oceans or mountains.	● Lake Ontario
COMPASS ROSE • A **compass rose** is a design on a map that assists the map reader in finding directions. A compass rose shows the four cardinal directions: north, south, east and west.	
SCALE • A **scale** is a bar on a map that resembles a ruler. The scale shows how a smaller distance is used to represent or show a larger distance. For example one centimeter on the map equals fifty kilometres in real life.	Scale/Echelle 0 100 200 300 km
SYMBOL • A **symbol** on a map is a picture that stands for something that is shown on a map.	Airport
LEGEND • The **map legend** tells the map reader what the symbols, colours and lines used on the map mean.	Map Legend ● City ★ Capital City

Map Breakdown

Choose a map and "breakdown" its parts.

What is the title of your map?	
Who might use this map and for what reason?	
What kind of things does this map show?	
Is there a compass rose? Explain.	
Does you map have a map key? Explain.	
Does your map show a scale? Explain.	

Map Grid: Campground

	1	2	3	4	5

A Map Grid

Manitoba

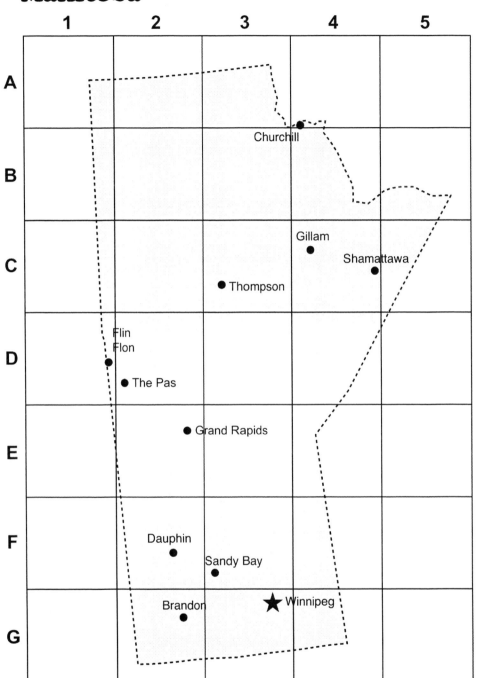

Map Legend
- ● City
- ★ Capital City

Brain Stretch

1. On a separate piece of paper, list the cities and tell their location on the map grid.

Map Grid

	1	2	3	4	5
A					
B					
C					
D					
E					

This is a Map of

Legend

Map Making Checklist

Name _____

Organization and Neatness • My work is neat and has detail. • My features can be clearly read. • I have a title for my map.	
Map Legend • I have a complete map legend.	
Scale • The features are drawn to scale.	
Spelling • I checked for spelling.	

Map Making Checklist

Name _____

Organization and Neatness • My work is neat and has detail. • My features can be clearly read. • I have a title for my map.	
Map Legend • I have a complete map legend.	
Scale • The features are drawn to scale.	
Spelling • I checked for spelling.	

Map Making Rubric

Student Name_____

	Level 1	Level 2	Level 3	Level 4
Organization and Neatness	Few of the labels or features can be clearly read.	Some of the labels or features can be clearly read.	Most of the labels or features can be clearly read.	Almost all of the labels or features can be clearly read.
Map Legend	The legend is missing or difficult to read.	The legend contains an incomplete set of symbols.	The legend contains a set of symbols.	The legend contains a thorough set of symbols.
Scale	Less than half of the features on the map are drawn to scale.	More than half of the features on the map are drawn to scale.	Most of the features on the map are drawn to scale.	Almost all of the features on the map are drawn to scale.
Spelling	Less than half of the words on the map are spelled correctly.	More than half of the words on the map are spelled correctly.	Most of the words on the map are spelled correctly.	Almost all of the words on the map are spelled correctly.

Teacher Comments

_____

_____

_____

More Activities...

A Map is a Flat Drawing of a Place

In a whole group setting, review with students how a map is a flat drawing of a place. Next, discuss with students how small things on a map represent large things in real life.

- With the guidance of the class, on chart paper draw a simple map of the classroom or schoolyard. The teacher may wish to talk about how symbols are used to represent different things on maps.
- Then have students draw a map of their own, such as their bedroom.

Globe and Maps

In a whole group setting, review with students what they know about a globe or world map. Brainstorm a list of types of information that people can get from these two things. Using a globe or world map have students find water and land.

Encourage students to notice that there is a world, and that:

- the world is made up of continents,
- those continents have countries within them
- those countries are divided up into smaller sections, such as provinces.

Challenge students by asking them to locate other countries, i.e.: where their families are from. The teacher may wish to keep track of the different countries by placing pins, or stars, etc. to mark locations.

Create Your Own Map

Have students create their own maps, such as:

- a map of the classroom
- a treasure map
- a map of mall
- a map of farm
- a map of the school yard
- a map of a zoo
- their route to go to school
- an amusement park

Atlas Scavenger Hunt

In whole group, review the different parts of an atlas and how it is useful. Next, have students take part in an "Atlas Scavenger Hunt". Look for places and things such as:

- cities
- provinces and territories
- lakes or rivers
- mountains
- oceans
- highways
- countries
- physical features

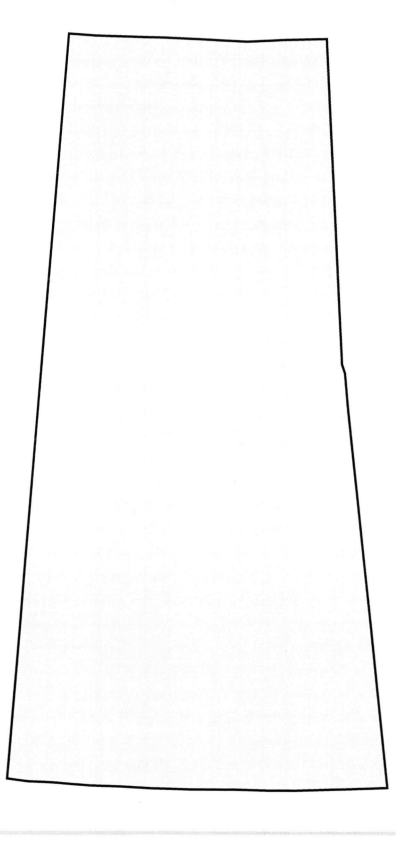

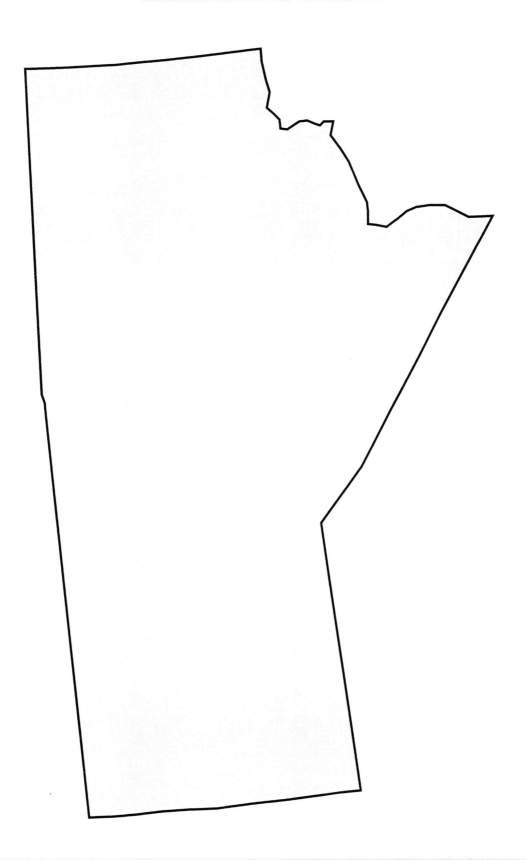

Québec

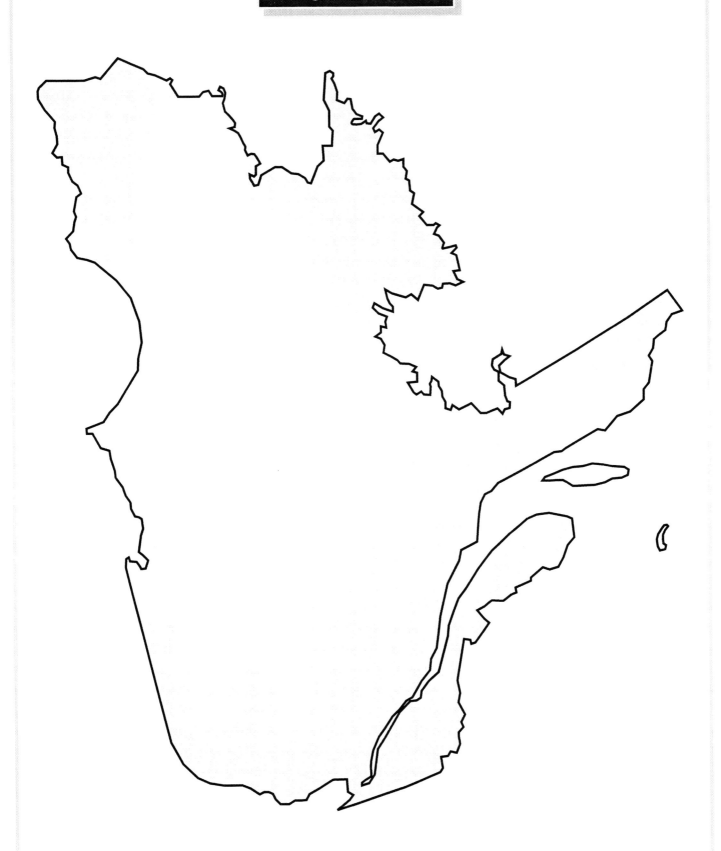

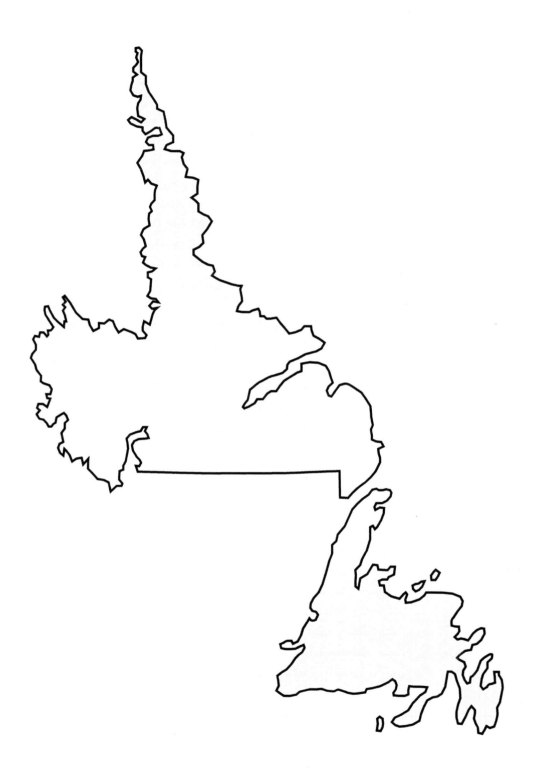

British Columbia

Scale/Echelle
0   100   200   300   400
km

Atlin
Atlin Lake
Stikine R
Fort Nelson
Stewart
Williston Lake
Hudson's Hope
Dawson Creek
Masset
Prince Rupert
Mackenzie
Queen Charlotte City
Fort St. James
Fraser Lake
Fl Fraser R
Queen Charlotte Islands
Bella Coola
Fraser R
Valemount
Kinbasket Lake
Williams Lake
Port McNeill
Port Alice
Lillooet
Ashcroft
Golden
Vancouver Island
Fl Columbia R
Penticton
Vancouver
Ucluelet
Cranbrook
Victoria

Map Legend
● City
★ Capital City

Alberta

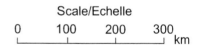

Scale/Echelle

0   100   200   300
|————|————|————|————| km

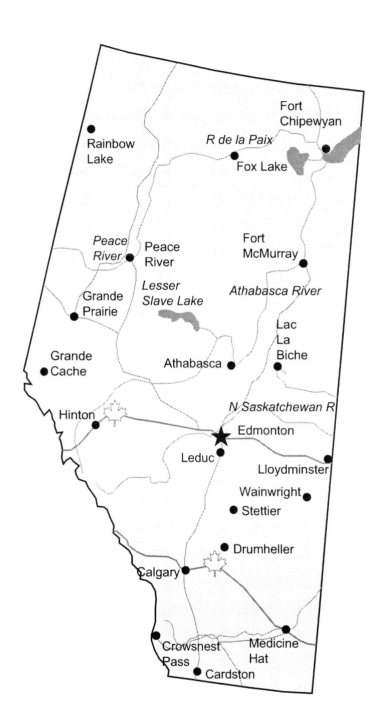

Rainbow Lake

Fort Chipewyan

R de la Paix

Fox Lake

Peace River   Peace River

Fort McMurray

Lesser Slave Lake   *Athabasca River*

Grande Prairie

Lac La Biche

Grande Cache

Athabasca

N Saskatchewan R

Hinton

Edmonton ★

Leduc

Lloydminster

Wainwright

Stettier

Drumheller

Calgary

Crowsnest Pass

Medicine Hat

Cardston

Map Legend

● City
★ Capital City

Saskatchewan

Fond-du-Lac

Lake Athabasca

Wollaston Lake

La Loche

Southend Reindeer

Churchill R.

Ild-a-la-Crosse

Pelican Narrows

La Ronge

Meadow Lake

Cumberland House

Prince Albert

North Battleford

Saskatchewan R.

Saskatoon

Yorkton

Saskatchewan R.

Regina

Swift Current

Maple Creek

Assinibola

Weyburn

Scale/Echelle

0   100   200   300
km

Map Legend

● City
★ Capital City

Manitoba

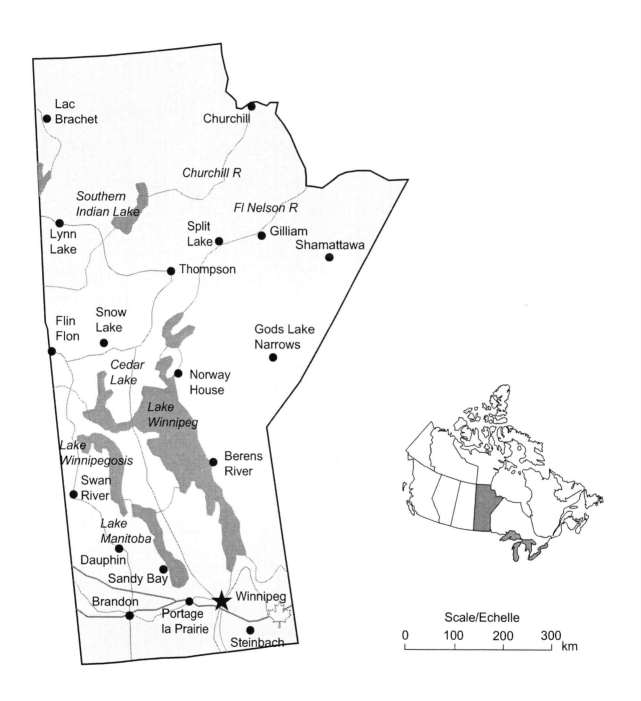

Lac Brachet

Churchill

Churchill R

Southern Indian Lake

Fl Nelson R

Lynn Lake

Split Lake

Gilliam

Shamattawa

Thompson

Snow Lake

Flin Flon

Gods Lake Narrows

Cedar Lake

Norway House

Lake Winnipeg

Lake Winnipegosis

Berens River

Swan River

Lake Manitoba

Dauphin

Sandy Bay

Brandon

Winnipeg

Portage la Prairie

Steinbach

Scale/Echelle

0   100   200   300
km

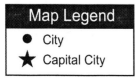

Map Legend

● City

★ Capital City

Ontario

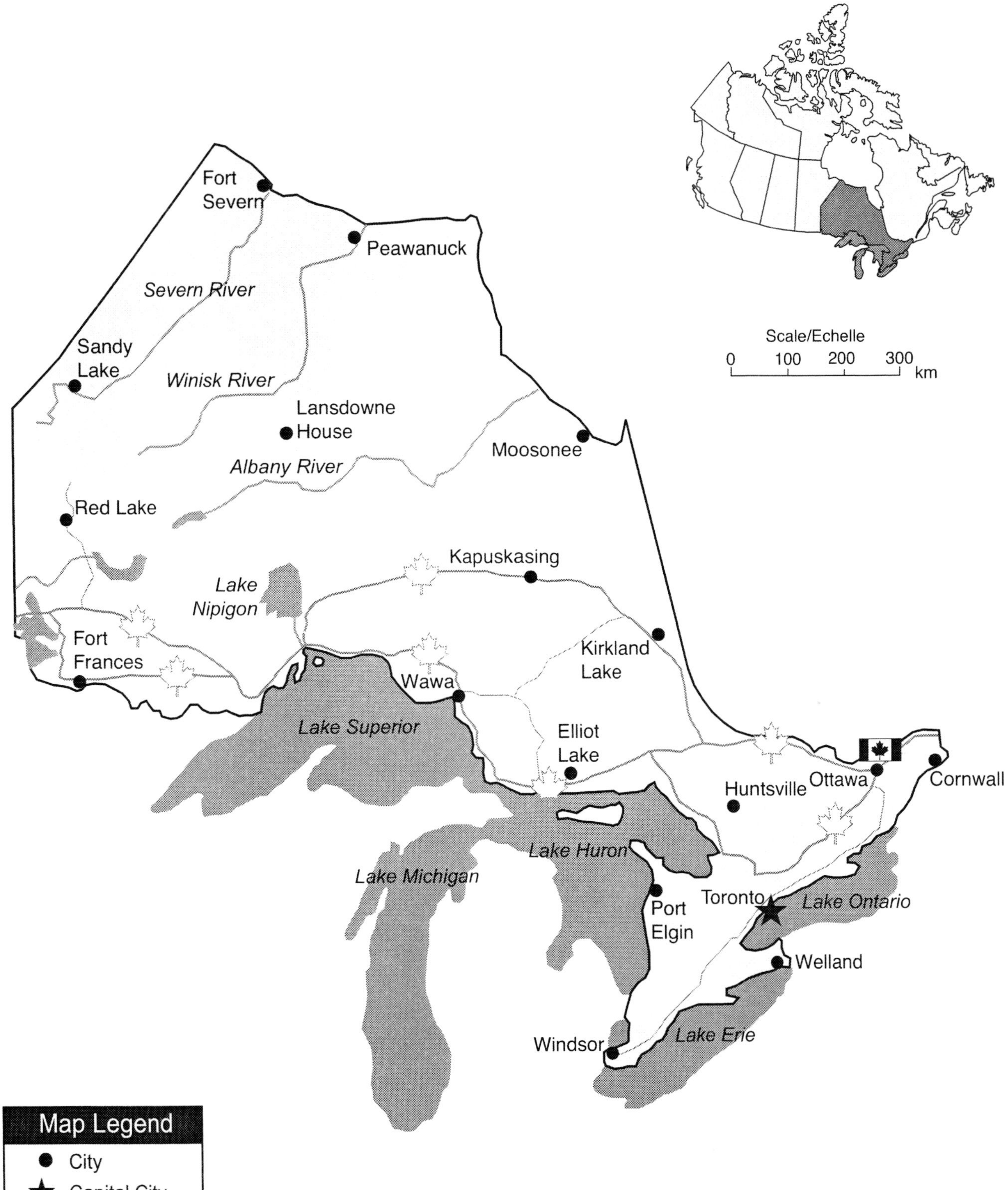

Fort Severn

Peawanuck

Severn River

Sandy Lake

Winisk River

Lansdowne House

Albany River

Moosonee

Red Lake

Kapuskasing

Lake Nipigon

Fort Frances

Kirkland Lake

Wawa

Lake Superior

Elliot Lake

Huntsville

Ottawa

Cornwall

Lake Huron

Lake Michigan

Toronto

Lake Ontario

Port Elgin

Welland

Windsor

Lake Erie

Scale/Echelle

0   100   200   300 km

Map Legend

● City

★ Capital City

Capital City of Canada

Québec

Salluit

PENINSULE
D'UNGAVA

Tasiujaq

La Riviere
aux Feuities

R Cantapiscau

Umiujaq

Hudson Bay

Reservoir de
Cantapiscau

Blanc
Sablon

La Grande Riviere

Fremont

Natashquan

R Romaine

Anticosti island

Eastmain

Lake
Mistassini

Port-
Cartier

Gulf of St. Lawrence

Gaspe

Matane

Iles de la
Madeleine

Mistissini

Matagami

Tadoussac

Amos

Quebec

Parent

Montmagny

Ville-Marie

Victoriaville

Montreal

Scale/Echelle

0   100   200   300
km

Map Legend
● City
★ Capital City

Newfoundland & Labrador

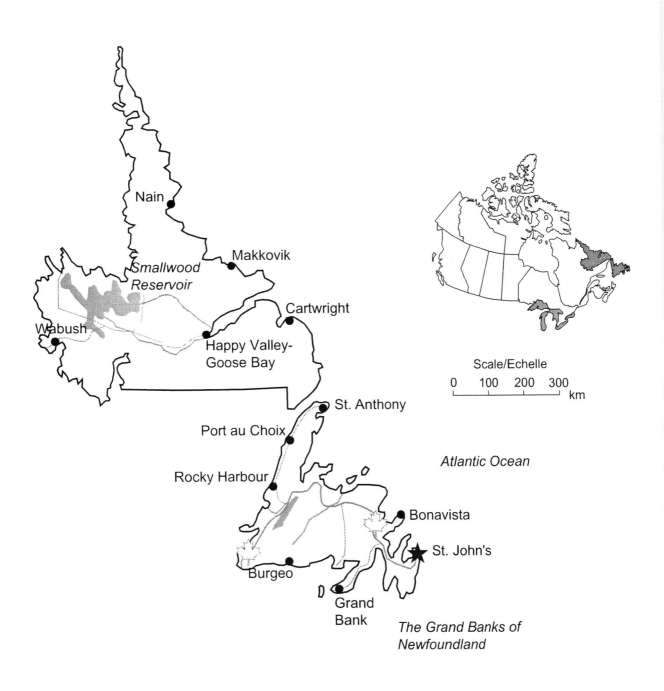

Scale/Echelle

0   100   200   300
km

Atlantic Ocean

The Grand Banks of
Newfoundland

Map Legend
- ● City
- ★ Capital City

New Brunswick

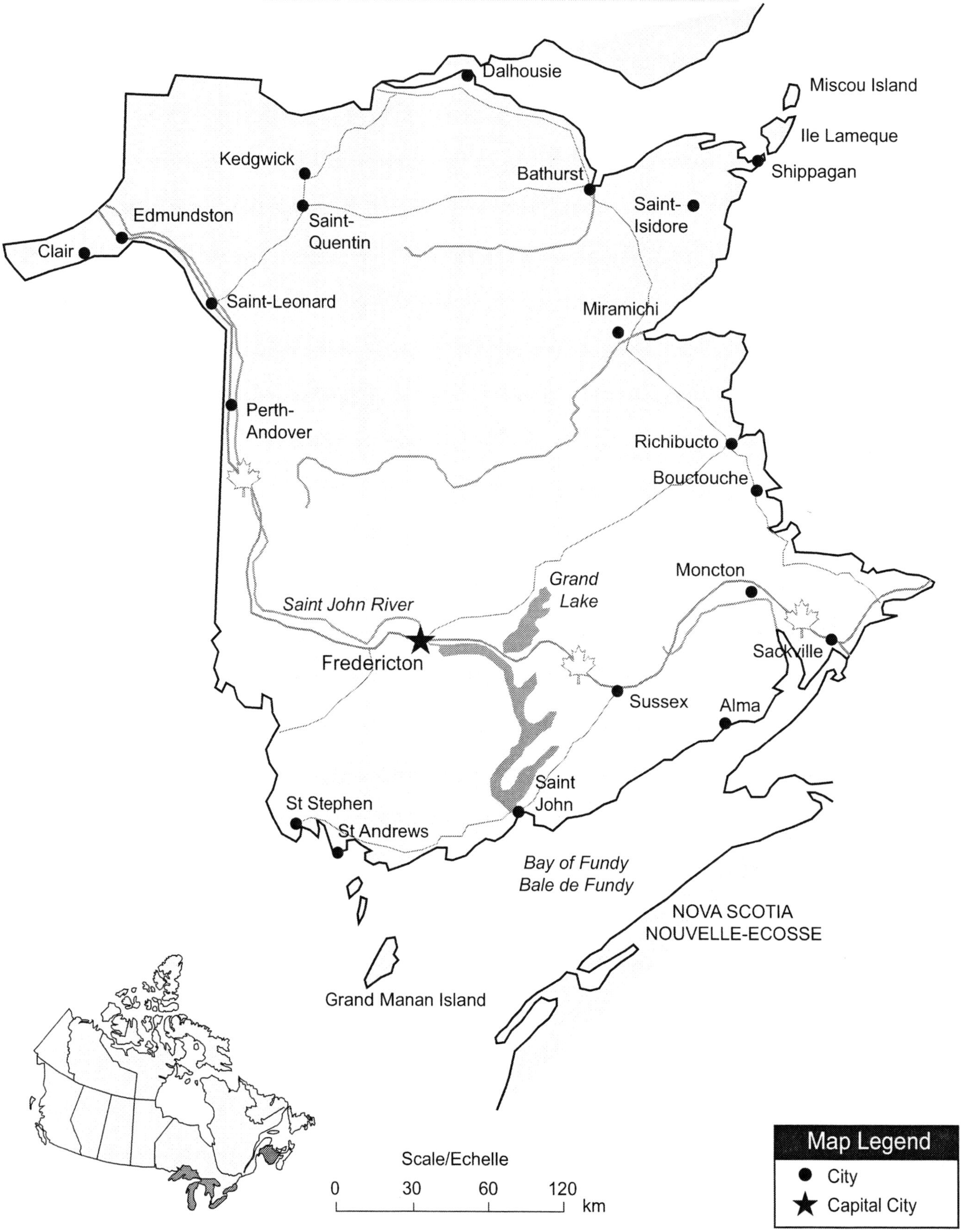

Dalhousie

Miscou Island

Ile Lameque

Kedgwick

Bathurst

Shippagan

Edmundston

Saint-Quentin

Saint-Isidore

Clair

Saint-Leonard

Miramichi

Perth-Andover

Richibucto

Bouctouche

Grand Lake

Moncton

Saint John River

Sackville

Fredericton

Sussex

Alma

St Stephen

St Andrews

Saint John

Bay of Fundy
Baie de Fundy

NOVA SCOTIA
NOUVELLE-ECOSSE

Grand Manan Island

Scale/Echelle

0   30   60   120
km

Map Legend

● City

★ Capital City

Prince Edward Island

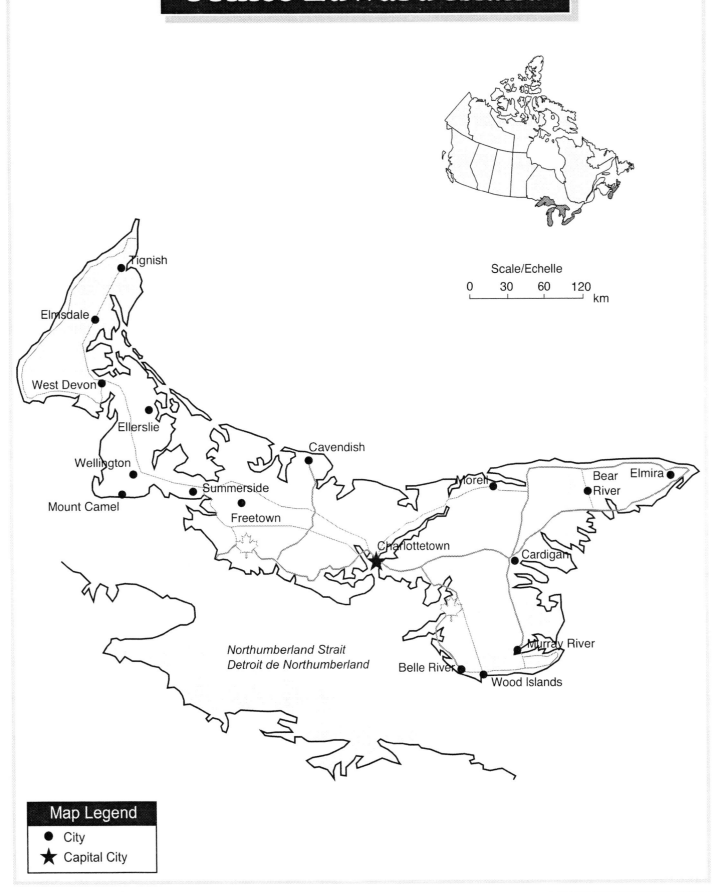

Scale/Echelle

0   30   60   120
km

Tignish

Elmsdale

West Devon

Ellerslie

Cavendish

Wellington

Morell

Bear River

Elmira

Summerside

Mount Camel

Freetown

Charlottetown

Cardigan

Northumberland Strait
Detroit de Northumberland

Murray River

Belle River

Wood Islands

Map Legend

● City

★ Capital City

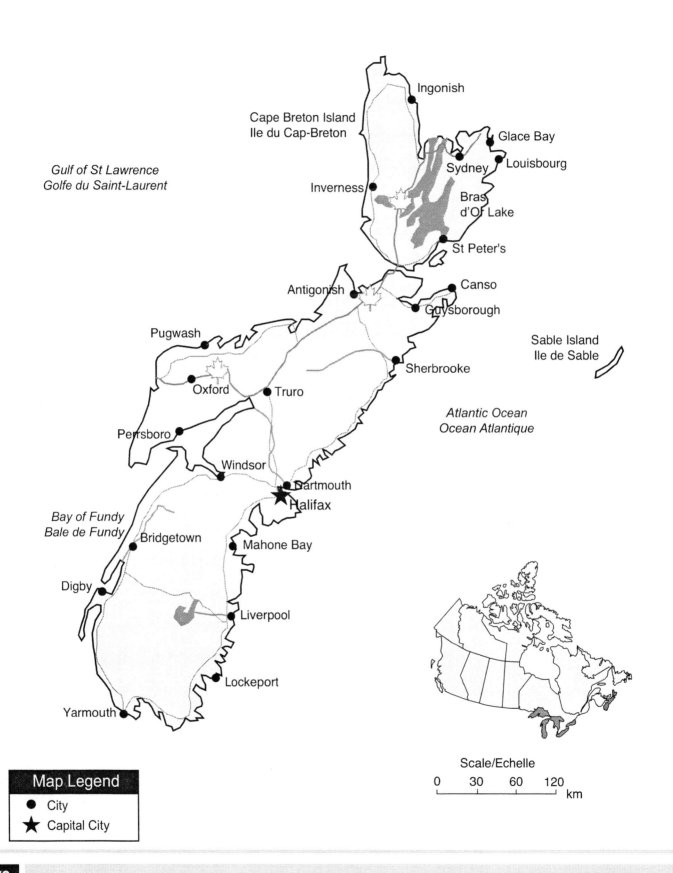

Ingonish

Cape Breton Island
Ile du Cap-Breton

Glace Bay

Sydney
Louisbourg

Gulf of St Lawrence
Golfe du Saint-Laurent

Inverness

Bras
d'OI Lake

St Peter's

Antigonish

Canso

Guysborough

Pugwash

Sable Island
Ile de Sable

Sherbrooke

Oxford
Truro

Atlantic Ocean
Ocean Atlantique

Perrsboro

Windsor

Dartmouth
Halifax

Bay of Fundy
Bale de Fundy

Bridgetown

Mahone Bay

Digby

Liverpool

Lockeport

Yarmouth

Scale/Echelle

0   30   60   120
                  km

Map Legend

● City
★ Capital City

Nunavut

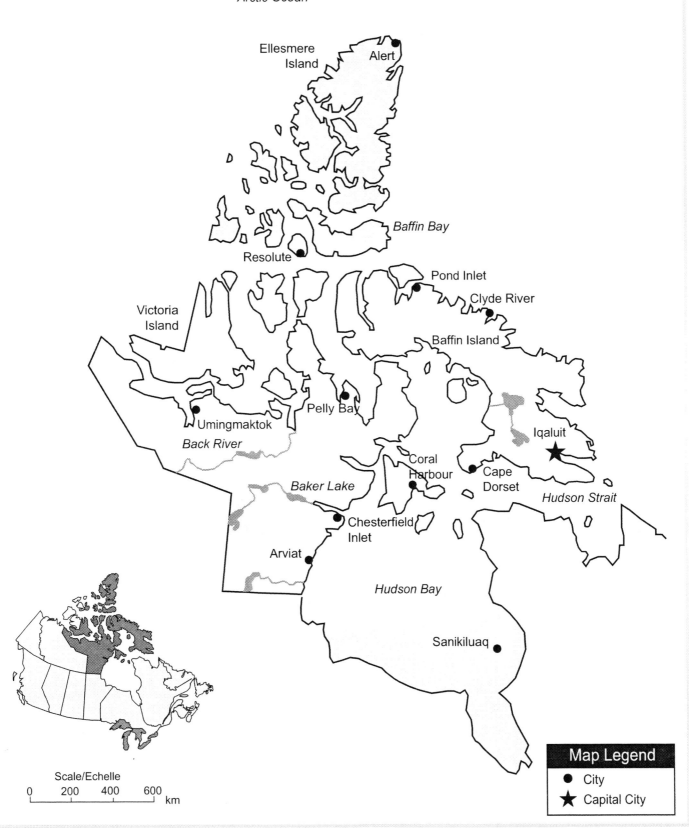

Arctic Ocean

Ellesmere Island

Alert

Baffin Bay

Resolute

Pond Inlet

Clyde River

Victoria Island

Baffin Island

Pelly Bay

Iqaluit

Umingmaktok

Back River

Coral Harbour

Cape Dorset

Baker Lake

Hudson Strait

Chesterfield Inlet

Arviat

Hudson Bay

Sanikiluaq

Map Legend

● City
★ Capital City

Scale/Echelle

0   200   400   600
                        km

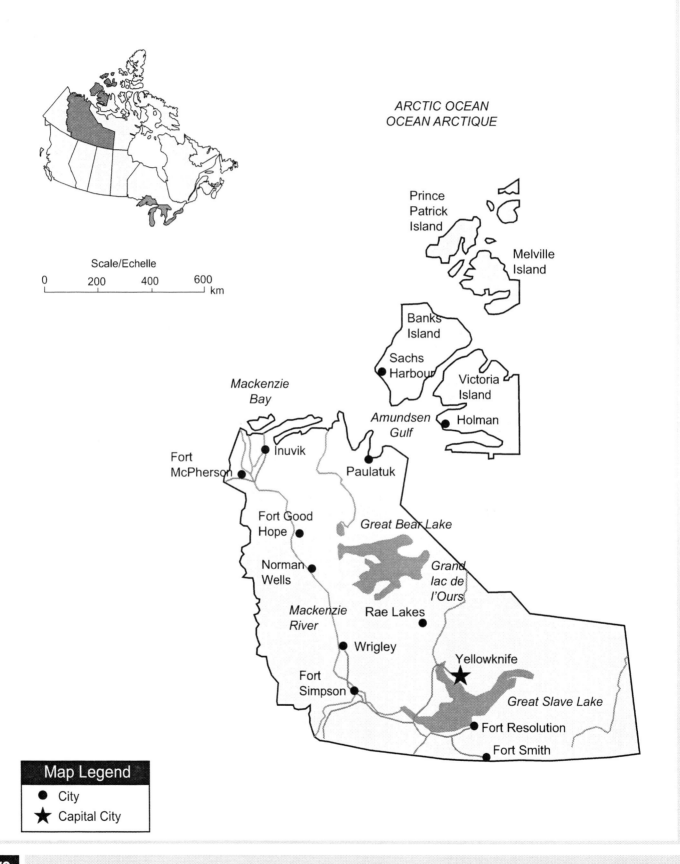

ARCTIC OCEAN
OCEAN ARCTIQUE

Prince
Patrick
Island

Melville
Island

Banks
Island

Sachs
Harbour

Victoria
Island

Holman

Scale/Echelle

0   200   400   600
                        km

Mackenzie
Bay

Amundsen
Gulf

Inuvik

Fort
McPherson

Paulatuk

Fort Good
Hope

Great Bear Lake

Norman
Wells

Grand
lac de
l'Ours

Mackenzie
River

Rae Lakes

Wrigley

Yellowknife

Fort
Simpson

Great Slave Lake

Fort Resolution

Fort Smith

Map Legend

● City

★ Capital City

Yukon Territory

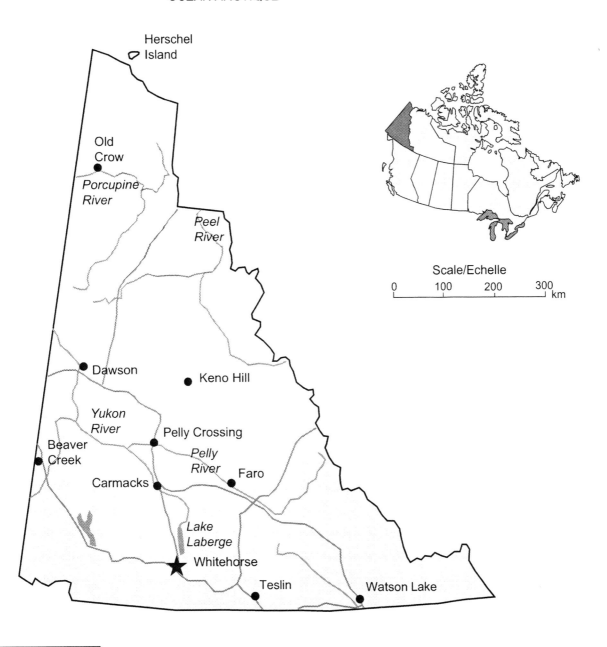

ARCTIC OCEAN
OCEAN ARCTIQUE

Herschel Island

Old Crow

Porcupine River

Peel River

Scale/Echelle

0   100   200   300
km

Dawson   Keno Hill

Yukon River

Pelly Crossing

Beaver Creek

Pelly River   Faro

Carmacks

Lake Laberge

Whitehorse

Teslin   Watson Lake

Map Legend

● City
★ Capital City

New Vocabulary

WORD	DEFINITION

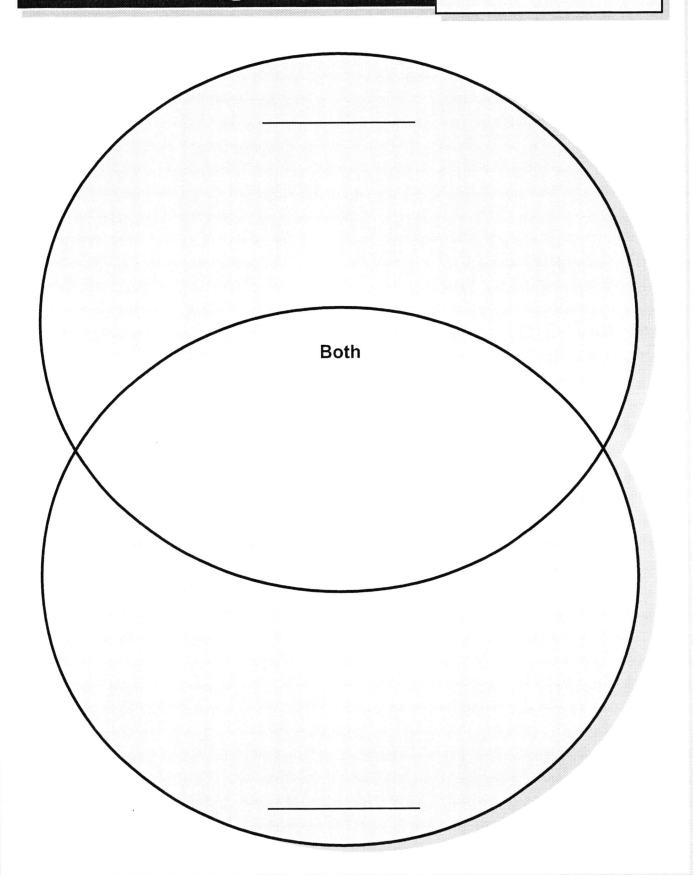

Both

A Comparison Chart About

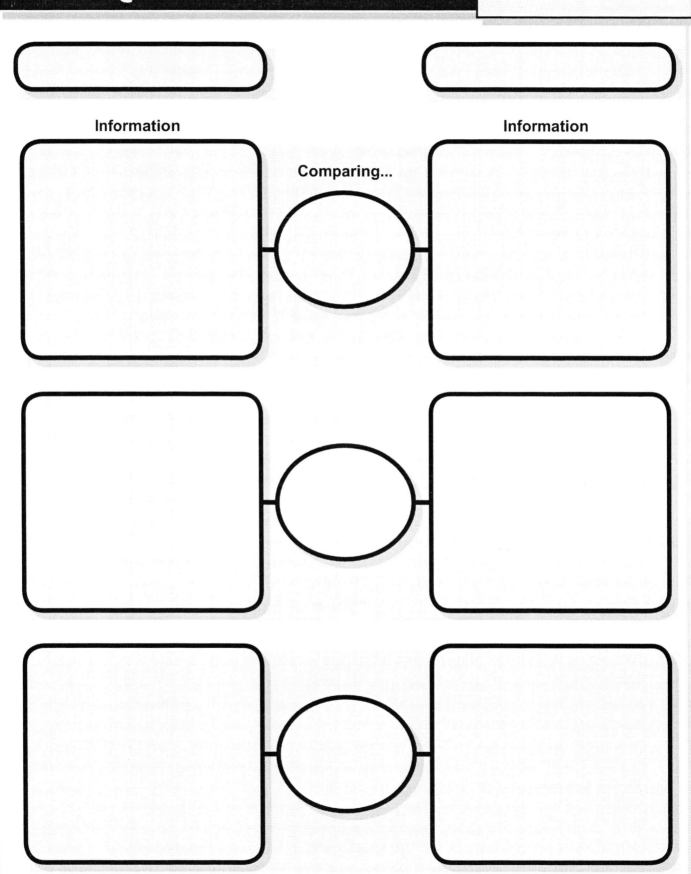

Information

Comparing...

Information

Student Participation Rubric

Level	Student Participation Descriptor
Level 4	Student consistently contributes to class discussions and activities by offering ideas and asking questions.
Level 3	Student usually contributes to class discussions and activities by offering ideas and asking questions.
Level 2	Student sometimes contributes to class discussions and activities by offering ideas and asking questions.
Level 1	Student rarely contributes to class discussions and activities by offering ideas and asking questions.

Understanding of Concepts Rubric

Level	Student Participation Descriptor
Level 4	Student shows a thorough understanding of all or almost all concepts and consistently gives appropriate and complete explanations independently. No teacher support is needed.
Level 3	Student shows a good understanding of most concepts and usually gives complete or nearly complete explanations. Infrequent teacher support is needed.
Level 2	Student shows a satisfactory understanding of most concepts and sometimes gives appropriate, but incomplete explanations. Teacher support is sometimes needed.
Level 1	Student shows little understanding of concepts and rarely gives complete explanations. Intensive teacher support is needed.

Communication of Concepts Rubric

Level	Student Participation Descriptor
Level 4	Student consistently communicates with clarity and precision in written and oral work. Student consistently uses appropriate terminology and vocabulary.
Level 3	Student usually communicates with clarity and precision in written and oral work. Student usually uses appropriate terminology and vocabulary.
Level 2	Student sometimes communicates with clarity and precision in written and oral work. Student sometimes uses appropriate terminology and vocabulary.
Level 1	Student rarely communicates with clarity and precision in written and oral work. Student rarely uses appropriate terminology and vocabulary.

Class Evaluation List

Student Name	Class Participation	Understanding of Concepts	Communication of Concepts	Overall Evaluation

SUPER GEOGRAPHER!

This award is for:

_____

MAP EXPERT

This award is for:

_____

http://atlas.gc.ca/site/english/learningresources/ccatlas/index.html

The Canadian Communities Atlas offers a unique national network of geographic information by providing schools the opportunity to create an internet-based atlas of their community.

http://www.ext.vt.edu/resources/4h/virtualfarm/main.html

This is an excellent website for students to explore different kinds of farming. By exploring this website students will gain a better understanding of how farming affects their daily lives.

http://www.whitebirch.ca/kids/kids.shtml

This is a great website sponsored by the Saskatchewan Forestry Association. This site provides interesting information about forestry and has a special section for kids.

http://www.cws-scf.ec.gc.ca/kids/index_e.cfm

At this Canadian wildlife service web site, students will learn about the endangered species in Canada, play games, and find out about acid rain and pollution.

http://www.aboriginalcanada.com/firstnation/

This is an informative website that allows you to navigate through a directory of several First Nations community websites.

http://www.lizardpoint.com/fun/geoquiz/canquiz.html

This is an interesting website where students can test their knowledge of where provinces and territories are located on a map.

http://ceps.statcan.ca/english/profil/placesearchform1.cfm

This government website allows students to find out information about communities across Canada. A mapping feature is also available.

http://www.canadiangeographic.ca/kidstest/

The Canadian Geographic For Kids website offers students numerous opportunities to learn about Canadian geography. This sites includes interactive educational games, an online atlas and much more!

http://pbskids.org/rogers/

The Mister Rogers Neighourhood website has sections where kids can build their own neighbourhood or take a factory tour to see how things are made.

http://www.nrcan.gc.ca/mms/wealth/intro-e.htm

This government website allows students to take a tour of spaces in the home and identifies minerals used in many household items.

http://www.viarail.ca/tourists/en_tour_phot.html

This website is a great resource for viewing photos of landscapes across Canada.